A Concise & Simple Guide to
Negotiation Techniques & Strategies

The Art of
NEGOTIATION

JOHN FRANCIS

The Art of Negotiation (First Edition)
Copyright © 2025 John Francis

Print ISBN: 978-1-7395212-2-6

Published in United Kingdom
by Sekal Publishing
All rights reserved.

This book is protected under the copyright laws. This book may not be copied or reprinted for commercial gain or profit.
The use of short quotations or occasional page copying for personal or group study is permitted and encouraged.
Permission will be granted upon request.

All Scripture quotations, unless otherwise indicated are taken from the Holy Bible, King James Version.

Graphic Design by Sekal Publishing

Other Titles by the Author

Is There A Word From the Lord?

What Do You Do When You're Left Alone?

10 Steps to Get Out of Debt

The Pastors & Church Workers Handbook

Talitha Cumi – Secrets of the Prayer Shawl

Walking In Your Assignment

For more information visit:

Website: www.johnfrancis.org.uk
Phone: Ruach City Church
+44 20 8678 6888
Email: global@ruachcitychurch.org
Facebook: BishopJohnFrancis
X (formerly known as Twitter): BishopJFrancis
Instagram: BishopJFrancis

About the Author

Bishop John Francis is a seasoned entrepreneur and a notable figure in the world of music and business. He embarked on his entrepreneurial journey at the young age of 16 with the establishment of his company, Opal Music. This innovative music and record company was dedicated to bridging the clear gap between the gospel and secular music industries, showcasing talented singers and bringing their inspirational messages to a broader audience. Under John's leadership, Opal Music also evolved into an agency for the renowned UK Inspirational Choir, further solidifying his influence in the music scene.

As a pioneer in the UK gospel music industry, John gained recognition not only for his business acumen but also for his role as a co-presenter on the London Weekend Television show "People Get Ready." His passion for music and community led him to establish the Ruach City Church, which quickly became one of the fastest-growing churches in the UK.

John began his journey into property negotiation with the acquisition of his church's first building in Brixton, purchased at auction. This pivotal moment set the stage for a series of successful negotiations, including the purchase of additional properties in Kilburn, Northwest London; in Birmingham, in Walthamstow East London; Streatham, Southwest London and an impressive 24 acres of land in Norbury. His visionary approach and negotiation skills has culminated in a joint venture to develop over 300 homes, including affordable housing, a sports complex, and a senior citizen home.

With a natural gift for negotiation, John has navigated the complexities of both personal and professional property deals, earning respect and admiration from peers and colleagues alike. Encouraged by many to share his insights and experiences—**"The Art of Negotiation"** is the result! He now invites readers to embark on their own journey and explore his new book **"The Art of Negotiation."**

Join John as he imparts the wisdom and the strategies he has learned over several decades to equip you with tools needed to thrive in your own negotiation endeavours.

Contents

About the Author	6
CHAPTER ONE: Understanding Negotiation	14
CHAPTER TWO The Art of Negotiation	22
CHAPTER THREE: Negotiation - Property Buying	34
CHAPTER FOUR: Negotiation - Property Selling	48
CHAPTER FIVE: Advanced Negotiation Techniques	60
Conclusion	70
Appendix 1 Resources for Further Reading	84

Appendix 2
Glossary of Negotiation Terms 85

Your Personal Negotiation Key Points 88

THE ART OF NEGOTIATION

A Concise & Simple Guide to
Negotiation Techniques & Strategies

The Art Of Negotiation

JOHN FRANCIS

CHAPTER 1
Understanding Negotiation

Negotiation is an art and a science, a dynamic tactical interplay of communication, persuasion, and strategy. At its core, negotiation is the process by which two or more parties come together to resolve differing interests, settle disputes or reach agreements. Many do not realise that it is a fundamental and normal aspect of human interaction, and it permeates every facet of our lives. Believe it or not, it can be seen in most of our personal relationships, corporate environments and can even feature in international diplomacy.

Definition of Negotiation

The simple definition of negotiation is 'discussion aimed at reaching an agreement.' As one considers negotiation in its broader sense and on more levels we find there is more to negotiation than meets the eye! Negotiation can be defined as the dialogue between two or more parties aimed at reaching a consensus or agreement. It involves a series of discussions where all participants express their needs, interests, and priorities to find common ground. Successful negotiation is not merely about winning or losing; instead, it is about collaboration and creating value for all involved. Whether it's haggling over a price at the local market, settling workplace disputes, or drafting treaties between nations, negotiation plays a pivotal role in shaping outcomes.

The negotiation process typically unfolds in several necessary stages: preparation, discussion, clarifying of goals, negotiation towards a win-win outcome, and closure. At each stage, one must very carefully consider the parties' objectives, the dynamics of the relationship, and the context of the negotiation itself. Possessing the ability to navigate these necessary stages effectively and strategically, is crucial for achieving favourable and desired results.

The Psychology Behind Negotiation

It is important for one to understand the psychological underpinnings of negotiation. In fact it is essential for anyone seeking to improve their skills in this area. Negotiation is not just about the facts of the matter; it is equally about emotions, perceptions, and cognitive biases that influence our decision-making processes.

One key psychological concept in negotiation is the idea of **"anchoring."** This phenomenon occurs when one party sets an initial offer that serves as a reference point for the rest of the negotiation.

Research shows that the first number put on the table can significantly affect the final outcome, often leading to a bias towards that initial figure.

Another important aspect is the role of **empathy**. This involves understanding the perspective of the other party which can create rapport and foster trust, making it more likely that a mutually beneficial agreement can be reached. Effective negotiators often employ active listening and emotional intelligence to gauge the other party's feelings and attitudes, which can guide their approach throughout the whole negotiation process.

Common Misconceptions

Despite its prevalence in our daily lives and interactions, many people hold misconceptions about negotiation that can hinder their effectiveness. One common myth is that negotiation is the same as or synonymous with conflict or confrontation. While it is true that negotiations can often involve instances of disagreement, they do not have to escalate into intense, uncomfortable or adversarial situations. In fact, the most successful negotiators view the process as a collaborative effort to address the needs of all parties involved.

Another misconception that we find is the assumption that negotiation is a zero-sum game, where one party's gain is inherently another's loss. In reality, when we look closely we find that many

> "One of the best ways to persuade others is by listening to them."
> — Dean Rusk

negotiations can result in win-win scenarios where both sides leave the table satisfied with the outcome. This mindset shift actually encourages creative problem-solving and can lead to innovative solutions that benefit all parties.

Finally, many individuals believe that negotiation is a talent reserved for a select few – the "natural born negotiators." In truth, negotiation is a skill that can be learned and honed through practice and experience. By understanding the principles outlined in this chapter and applying them in real-world situations, anyone can become a more effective negotiator.

As we delve deeper into the intricacies of negotiation in the subsequent chapters, we will explore specific strategies, techniques, and case studies that illustrate how these concepts come to life in various contexts. Whether you are negotiating a salary increase, a business deal, or a personal agreement, the knowledge gained in this chapter will serve as a solid foundation for your journey into the world of negotiation.

CHAPTER 2
The Art of Negotiation

Negotiation is often characterised as an art form, blending creativity with strategy to achieve desired outcomes. While there are established techniques and theories that inform effective negotiation, the mastery of negotiation lies in the application of key skills, the nuances of communication, and the thoroughness of preparation. In this chapter, we will explore these essential elements that contribute to becoming a skilled negotiator.

Key Negotiation Skills

To navigate the complexities of negotiation successfully, several key skills are paramount. These skills not only enhance one's ability to negotiate effectively but also foster stronger relationships and better outcomes.

1. Active Listening

One of the most crucial skills in negotiation is the ability to listen actively. This goes beyond simply hearing the words spoken; it involves understanding the emotions and motivations behind those words. By demonstrating a genuine interest in the other party's perspective, negotiators can build rapport and create an environment conducive to collaboration.

2. Emotional Intelligence
A high level of emotional intelligence allows negotiators to manage their own emotions while also being attuned to the feelings of others. This skill is vital in recognising non-verbal cues, understanding when tensions rise, and responding appropriately to maintain a positive atmosphere.

3. Persuasion
The ability to persuade is at the heart of negotiation. Effective negotiators can present their case clearly and compellingly, using logic, emotion, and credibility to influence the other party's view or perception. Persuasion also involves identifying the interests of the other party and framing proposals in a way that aligns with their goals.

4. Problem-Solving

Negotiation often involves finding creative solutions to complex problems. Skilled negotiators view challenges as opportunities to innovate and also collaborate. They approach negotiations with a mindset geared towards brainstorming and generating options that satisfy both parties' interests.

5. Flexibility and Adaptability

No negotiation unfolds exactly as planned or expected. The ability to remain flexible and adapt to changing circumstances, new information, or unexpected reactions is crucial. Successful negotiators know when to pivot their strategy and when to stand firm, balancing assertiveness with openness.

6. Assertiveness

While collaboration is essential, being assertive is equally important. The quality of assertiveness allows negotiators to express their own desired needs and boundaries confidently. This skill ensures that one's interests are not being overlooked or ignored whilst in the pursuit of compromise.

The Role of Communication

Communication is the lifeblood of negotiation. How negotiators express themselves and correctly interpret or incorrectly interpret the messages of others can significantly impact the process and final outcome. Effective communication encompasses both verbal and non-verbal elements.

1. Clarity and Conciseness
Clear and concise communication helps to avoid misunderstandings and any confusion. When presenting and articulating proposals, negotiators should aim to be straightforward, using simple language and ensuring they avoid jargon and clichés that may alienate the other party and cloud the negotiation process.

2. Non-Verbal Communication
Body language, tone of voice, and facial expressions can convey emotions and intentions as powerfully as words. Being aware of one's own non-verbal signals and being able to read those of others can provide valuable insights into the negotiation dynamics.

3. Questioning Techniques
The use of questions can facilitate dialogue and uncover valuable information. Open-ended questions often promote and encourage discussion, while closed questions can clarify specifics. Using strategic questioning helps negotiators gather insights into the other party's interests, expected outcomes and preferences.

4. Feedback
Providing and soliciting feedback during negotiation helps to ensure that both parties are on the same page. It fosters transparency and allows for adjustments to be made in real-time, which promotes a more collaborative atmosphere.

The Importance of Preparation

Preparation is the main cornerstone of successful negotiation. A well-prepared negotiator has a clear understanding of their own objectives, as well as insights into the other party's interests and potential motivations. Preparation involves several key components:

1. Research

Gathering relevant information about key areas such as the other party, industry standards, and market conditions is essential. Knowledge empowers negotiators to make informed decisions and strengthens their position.

2. Setting Objectives

Clear goals are vital for guiding the negotiation process. Negotiators should establish their ideal outcome, as well as their minimum acceptable terms. This clarity provides a roadmap for discussions and helps negotiators recognize when to compromise.

3. Developing Strategies
Effective negotiators outline their strategies and tactics in advance. This includes anticipating possible objections at every stage, thinking about and preparing for counterarguments and formulating creative solutions that address the interests of both parties.

4. Role-Playing
Engaging in role-playing exercises can help negotiators practice their skills and refine their strategies. Simulating and practicing different scenarios can build and instil confidence and prepare negotiators for a range of responses.

5. Contingency Planning
No negotiation is without risk. Preparing for potential obstacles and developing and preparing contingency plans ensures that negotiators are equipped to handle unexpected developments without losing sight of their objectives.

> "Negotiations are worthless if neither party is willing to budge."
> — Dave Waters

In conclusion, the art of negotiation is a multifaceted skill that can be learnt by one who is committed. It encompasses the following actions: refining essential abilities, intentional and effective communication and practicing thorough preparation. By sharpening these skills and embracing the principles outlined in this chapter, negotiators can enhance their effectiveness and achieve more favourable outcomes.

In the following chapters, we will delve deeper into specific proven negotiation techniques, strategies, and look at real-life examples to further enrich your understanding of this vital art.

CHAPTER 3
Negotiation - Property Buying

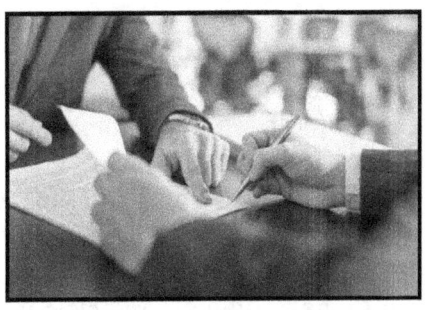

The property market is a complex and dynamic landscape where negotiation plays a pivotal role in achieving the best possible outcomes for buyers and sellers alike. Understanding the nuances of this market, mastering the art of negotiating a buying price and learning from real-life case studies can empower prospective homeowners and investors to make informed decisions. In this chapter, we will explore the critical aspects of property buying negotiation.

Understanding the Property Market
Before entering a negotiation, it is essential to have a complete and thorough understanding and correct knowledge of the property market. This knowledge provides a foundation for effective negotiations and allows buyers to make educated decisions.

1. Market Trends
Property markets fluctuate based on various factors, including economic conditions, interest rates, demand, and supply. Staying informed about current market trends can help buyers identify opportune moments to negotiate. For instance, a buyer may have better leverage in a buyer's market, where

supply exceeds demand, compared to a seller's market characterised by high competition.

2. Property Valuation
Understanding how properties are valued is crucial. Factors such as location, size, condition, and comparable sales (comps) in the area play significant roles in determining a property's worth. A thorough appraisal can provide insights into whether a property is fairly priced, allowing buyers to negotiate from a position of strength.

3. Local Regulations
Familiarity with property taxes, local real estate regulations and planning/zoning laws can influence negotiations. Buyers should be aware of any restrictions that may affect their

intended use of the property, as well as any potential costs involved in renovations or compliance.

4. Market Sentiment

The emotional dynamics of the market can impact negotiations. It is very important to understand the motivations of sellers — whether they are eager to sell quickly or are willing to wait for the best offer. This information can contribute to a buyer's strategy. In addition, recognising the psychological factors at play can help buyers tailor their negotiation approach.

How to Negotiate a Buying Price

Negotiating a buying price in property transactions requires a blend of the following: strategy, communication, and emotional intelligence.

THE ART OF NEGOTIATION

Here are 7 steps to effectively negotiate a favourable price:

1. Do Your Homework
Knowledge is power. Before entering negotiations, one should conduct a thorough research on the specific property and the market. Identify comparable properties that have sold recently to establish a fair price range. This data will provide a solid basis for your negotiations.

2. Set Your Budget and Goals
Determine your maximum budget and desired price range before negotiations begin. Having clear financial boundaries helps prevent emotional decision-making during the negotiation process.

3. Build Rapport with the Seller
Establishing a positive relationship with the seller or their agent can create a more conducive negotiating environment. Find common ground and demonstrate genuine interest in the property. This rapport can lead to more favourable terms.

4. Start with a Reasonable Offer
Providing an initial offer that is below the asking price can be an effective tactic, but ensure that it is reasonable based on your research. An excessively low offer may alienate the seller, while a fair offer shows that you are serious while still seeking value.

5. Be Prepared to Justify Your Offer
When presenting your offer, be ready to explain the rationale behind it. Reference your market research and

any comparable sales that support your proposal. This transparency on your part can strengthen your position and encourage the seller to consider your offer seriously.

6. Be Flexible and Open to Compromise
Negotiation is a two-way street. Be willing to listen to the seller's perspective and consider their needs. Flexibility in terms of closing dates, contingencies, or minor repairs can create goodwill and facilitate a more successful negotiation.

7. Use Time to Your Advantage
Timing can be a powerful negotiation tool. If the seller has been on the market for an extended period or is facing financial pressures, they may be more willing to negotiate. Conversely, if the property is receiving

multiple offers, you may need to act quickly and decisively.

Case Studies of Successful Property Buying Negotiations

To illustrate the key principles of negotiation in property buying, let's examine a couple of case studies that highlight effective strategies and outcomes.

Case Study 1:
The First-Time Buyer

Sarah, a first-time homebuyer, was interested in a charming bungalow in a lovely desirable neighbourhood. After conducting thorough research about sales of properties in the area, she discovered that similar properties had recently sold for £250,000 to £275,000. The asking price for the bungalow was £299,000, and it had been on the market for over three months.

Armed with data from comparable sales, Sarah made an initial offer of £240,000. Although the seller was initially taken aback, Sarah presented her market research and explained her reasoning. The seller ultimately countered with a price of £270,000. The result — Sarah, had established a rapport with the seller and recognising their motivation to sell, agreed to a final price of £260,000, successfully negotiating a deal below the original asking price.

Case Study 2:
The Investor's Strategy

Jim, a seasoned real estate investor, targeted a multi-family property that had been on the market for a while. He recognised that the seller was facing financial difficulties and was motivated to sell really quickly. Jim decided to conduct a comprehensive research and identified that the property needed significant repairs, which he used to his advantage.

Knowing the market value of the property in its current condition was around £400,000, Jim began negotiations with an offer of £360,000. He justified his offer by outlining the costs of necessary repairs and renovations. After some back-and-forth dialogue, Jim and the seller settled on a final price of £375,000, allowing both parties to leave the negotiation satisfied.

These case studies underscore the importance of the key principles of preparation, research, communication,

THE ART OF NEGOTIATION

and emotional intelligence in the negotiation process. By applying these principles, buyers can navigate the property market with confidence and achieve favourable outcomes.

In the chapters that follow, we'll look further into advanced negotiation techniques and explore strategies for specific scenarios, ensuring you are well-equipped and ready for any future negotiation situation that comes your way.

Buying at Auction in the UK & USA
Buying property at auction can be an exhilarating and strategic way to secure a home or investment property, whether in the UK or the USA. In the UK, you will find that property auctions are conducted by auction houses, where buyers can bid on residential

and commercial properties. It's crucial for bidders to carry out a thorough research prior to the day of the auction, including carrying out a property viewing or inspection. You should also read, take note of and ensure you understand the legal terms specified and outlined in the documentation provided in the auction pack.

> "Successful negotiation is not about getting to 'yes'; it's about mastering 'no' and understanding what the path to an agreement is."
> — Christopher Voss

In the USA, real estate auctions can take place both at the county level and through private auction houses. Buyers often have the opportunity to bid on foreclosures or distressed properties. Similar to the UK, due diligence is essential, as properties are typically sold "as is," meaning buyers must be prepared to handle any repairs or issues post-purchase.

In both markets, effective bidding strategies, such as setting a maximum bid beforehand and remaining calm under pressure, can significantly enhance the likelihood of a successful purchase. Additionally, understanding the auction process, including the terms of sale, buyer's premiums, and deposit requirements, are vital for navigating this unique buying experience.

CHAPTER 4
Negotiation - Property Selling

Selling property is not just a transaction; it is a strategic endeavour that requires careful planning and negotiation skills. Whether you are a seasoned real estate investor or a homeowner selling for the first time, understanding how to prepare your property for sale, negotiate effectively, and learn from successful case studies can make a significant difference in your selling experience. In this chapter, we will explore these key aspects of property selling negotiation.

Preparing Your Property for Sale
Preparation is crucial when it comes to selling property. A well-prepared property not only attracts potential buyers but also enhances your negotiation position. Here are some essential steps to consider:

1. Curb Appeal
First impressions matter. Invest time and effort into improving the exterior of your property. Simple upgrades like landscaping, painting the front door, and cleaning windows can create a welcoming atmosphere that draws potential buyers in.

2. Decluttering and Staging

A cluttered space can deter buyers and make it difficult for them to envision themselves in the home. Declutter each room, removing personal items and excess furniture. Consider staging the property to highlight its best features, making it more appealing and spacious. Property staging, also known as home staging, is the process of preparing a property for sale by making it look as appealing as possible to potential buyers. This involves all the above but you can also consider accessorizing to create a much more desirable living space.

> "The most difficult thing in any negotiation, almost, is making sure that you strip it of the emotion and deal with the facts."
> — Howard Baker

3. Repairs and Upgrades
Address and carry out any necessary repairs before listing the property. This could include fixing leaky faucets, patching holes in walls, or updating outdated fixtures. Minor upgrades, such as a fresh coat of paint or new appliances, etc. can significantly enhance the property's value and desirability.

4. Professional Photography
In today's digital age, high-quality photographs are essential for attracting buyers. Consider hiring a professional photographer to capture your property in the best light. Stunning images can make your listing stand out in a competitive market.

5. Gather Documentation
Prepare a comprehensive presentation

package with documentation related to the property you are selling. It should include accurate maintenance records, warranties, and disclosures. Having this information readily available can instill confidence in potential buyers and streamline the negotiation process.

6. Market Research
Understanding the local real estate market is vital for setting an appropriate asking price. Research comparable properties (comps) in your area, considering factors such as size, condition, and recent sales. This data will help you make an informed decision about your property's value.

How to Negotiate a Selling Price
Negotiating a selling price involves a careful balance of strategy and communication. Here are some steps

to effectively negotiate your selling price:

1. Set a Realistic Asking Price
Based on your market research, set an asking price that reflects the property's value while remaining competitive. An overpriced property can deter potential buyers, while an underpriced one may lead to missed opportunities.

2. Be Open to Offers
When you receive an offer, approach it with an open mind. Consider the buyer's perspective and evaluate the merits of their offer. A strong initial offer may warrant further negotiation, while a low-ball offer can be a starting point for discussion.

3. Know Your Bottom Line
Before negotiations begin, establish your minimum acceptable price. This clarity will help you navigate offers and counteroffers without losing sight of your goals.

4. Highlight Property Strengths
During negotiations, emphasise the unique features and strengths of your property. Discuss recent upgrades, the neighbourhood's amenities, and the overall appeal of the area. This narrative can help justify your asking price and persuade buyers of its value.

5. Stay Calm and Professional
Negotiations can become emotional, especially in a case where either party has some significant financial stakes involved. You should do your best to maintain a calm, focused and

professional state or demeanour, focusing on the facts rather than personal feelings. This approach fosters a positive and much more productive atmosphere.

6. Be Willing to Compromise

Flexibility is key in negotiation. Be open to options and offers to compromise that can benefit both parties, i.e. you can meet the buyer halfway on the price or offer to cover closing costs in exchange for a quicker sale. Creative solutions can lead to successful agreements.

Case Studies of Successful Property Selling Negotiations

To illustrate effective negotiation strategies in property selling, consider the following case studies.

Case Study 1:
The Renovated Townhouse

Lisa owned a townhouse in a desirable urban neighbourhood. After conducting market research, she determined that similar properties were selling for around £450,000. To enhance her property's appeal, she invested in repairs and minor renovations, including updated kitchen cabinets and new flooring.

When Lisa received an offer of £425,000, she felt it was too low. Instead of dismissing it outright, she engaged in a conversation with the prospective buyer. She highlighted the renovation works carried out and also the property's prime location. After some back and forth, they settled on a final price of £440,000, successfully leveraging the recent improvements to justify a higher selling price.

Case Study 2:
The Motivated Seller

Tom inherited a property that he needed to sell quickly due to financial circumstances. He researched his local market and found that similar homes were selling for approximately £300,000. However, he was motivated to close the deal quickly.

Tom listed the property at £290,000, knowing it was below market value but positioning himself for a quick sale. He received multiple offers within a week, with one buyer offering £295,000. Tom recognised the competitive environment and he decided to counter at £300,000, leveraging the interest he generated. The buyer accepted,

THE ART OF NEGOTIATION

and Tom was able to close the sale in record time.

These case studies underscore the importance of the key principles of preparation, communication and negotiation strategy in property selling. By applying these principles, sellers can navigate the complexities of the market and achieve successful outcomes.

CHAPTER 5
Advanced Negotiation Techniques

As we progress in our understanding of negotiation, it becomes essential to explore advanced strategies, deal with difficult negotiations and understand the role of a negotiator in property transactions. This chapter will equip you with sophisticated tools and insights to enhance your negotiation prowess.

Advanced Strategies for Negotiation

1. Interest-Based Negotiation: Rather than focusing solely on positions (the stated demands), explore the underlying interests of both parties. By understanding what each party truly values, you can identify creative solutions that satisfy both sides, leading to win-win outcomes.

2. BATNA (Best Alternative to a Negotiated Agreement): Knowing your BATNA gives you leverage in negotiations. It represents the best option you have if negotiations fail. The stronger your BATNA, the more confident you can become during negotiations, allowing you to walk away if necessary.

3. Negotiation Anchoring: Utilise the anchoring effect by setting an initial offer that influences the negotiation range. By starting with a number that aligns with your objectives, you can shape the conversation and the expectations of the other party.

4. The Power of Silence: Silence can be a powerful negotiation tool. After making an offer or presenting a point, resist the urge to fill the silence. Allow the other party time to process the information, which can lead to more thoughtful responses.

5. Use of Time: Be mindful of timing in negotiations. Knowing when to push for a decision and when to give space can affect the outcome. For instance, if a buyer is eager to close, you may have more leverage to negotiate favourable terms.

Dealing with Difficult Negotiations
Negotiations can become challenging for various reasons, including emotional tensions, differing priorities, or complex issues. Here are strategies to navigate difficult negotiations effectively:

1. Stay Calm and Composed: In challenging situations, maintaining your composure is critical. Take deep breaths, and don't let emotions dictate your responses. A calm demeanour can help de-escalate tensions and foster a more productive dialogue.

2. Focus on Common Goals: Redirect the conversation key points towards shared and established objectives. Emphasising common ground can help both parties see the value in collaboration and reduce *adversarial* attitudes.

3. Ask Open-Ended Questions: Encourage dialogue by asking open-ended questions that invite the other party to share their perspective. This approach can reveal underlying concerns and facilitate more constructive discussions.

4. Practice Active Listening: You can demonstrate that you value the other party's input by actively listening to their concerns. Acknowledging their feelings can build rapport and create a more positive amicable negotiating environment.

5. Know When to Walk Away: Sometimes, the best option is to walk away from a negotiation that is no longer serving your interests. Knowing your limits and being willing to step back can prevent you from making concessions and/or that undermine your objectives and change your original negotiation focus.

The Role of a Negotiator in Property Transactions

In property transactions, the role of a negotiator is multifaceted and essential. Whether you are negotiating on your own behalf or working with a real estate agent, understanding this role can enhance your negotiation effectiveness.

1. Facilitator of Communication: Negotiators serve as intermediaries between buyers and sellers, facilitating communication to ensure that both parties understand each other's perspectives and needs.

2. Advocate for Interests: A skilled negotiator advocates for their client's best interests, ensuring that their objectives are prioritised throughout the negotiation process.

3. Problem Solver: Negotiators often encounter challenges that require creative solutions. They must think critically and collaboratively to find mutually beneficial outcomes that satisfy both parties.

4. Emotional Regulator: Negotiators help manage the emotional dynamics of the negotiation process. By maintaining a level-headed approach, they can defuse tensions, create a positive environment and promote constructive dialogue.

5. Strategic Planner: Effective negotiators develop strategies that align with their clients' goals. They anticipate potential obstacles and prepare for various scenarios, allowing them to adapt as negotiations evolve.

In conclusion, advanced negotiation techniques, the ability to handle difficult and challenging negotiations and understanding the role of a negotiator are crucial for success in property transactions. By mastering these elements, you can enhance your negotiation skills and achieve favourable outcomes.

As we draw this exploration of negotiation to a close, it's essential to recap the key insights and strategies discussed throughout the book. Negotiation is a vital and much needed skill that permeates every aspect of property transactions, from buying and selling to navigating complex scenarios.

We have examined the foundations of negotiation, focusing on understanding the market, preparing for negotiations, and employing effective strategies. We delved into the intricacies of property buying and selling, providing you with practical tips and case studies to illustrate successful negotiation techniques.

> "Information is a negotiator's greatest weapon."
> —Victor Kiam

Looking to the future, the landscape of negotiation in property transactions is evolving with new and innovative technological advances and shifts in market dynamics, the ability to adapt and refine negotiation skills will remain paramount.

Embracing new tools and methods will empower negotiators to navigate the complexities of the real estate market successfully.

Conclusion

The Wisdom of Proverbs 23 in Business Negotiation

Proverbs 23:1-3
When you sit down to dine with a ruler, carefully consider what is in front of you. Place a knife at your throat to control your appetite. Don't long for the ruler's delicacies;
the food misleads.

Proverbs 23 offers profound wisdom that can be applied to the realm of business negotiation, particularly in the context of dealing with powerful or influential figures. The opening verses advise us to *"consider diligently what is before thee"* when dining with a ruler, which serves as a metaphor for engaging with those in positions of authority or influence. In a business setting, this translates to the importance of being mindful and strategic when entering negotiations with powerful stakeholders or decision-makers. The metaphorical approach to this verse can also imply that you should do your homework! What do you know about them? How have they conducted themselves in other negotiation scenarios? How investigated are they in negotiating to a satisfactory resolution? Do they really want to sell, merge, do a deal? What is the current financial state of the company/organization?

The subsequent admonition to *"put a knife to thy throat"* if one is prone to excessive appetite underscores the necessity of self-control and discipline. For business professionals, this means being aware of their desires and ambitions, particularly in high-stakes negotiations where the allure of immediate gains can cloud judgment and open you to accepting terms that are far from your original goals. Maintaining a level of restraint and focusing on long-term objectives rather than succumbing to impulsive decisions is crucial for sustainable success.

Ultimately, this proverb remind us that in the world of business, wisdom, awareness, and self-discipline are essential tools for navigating negotiations and forging fruitful partnerships.

King Solomon
– A Shrewd Businessman

The Book of Proverbs is part of the wisdom literature in the Hebrew Bible, known for its insightful sayings and teachings on how to live a wise life. It is traditionally ascribed to King Solomon, although not all of its contents are necessarily written by him. It is believed that he compiled or collected some. We know that Solomon wrote 3,000 proverbs and 1,005 songs (1 Kings 4:32) so generally the first portion of the book of Proverbs is attributed to him (specifically Proverbs chapters 1 – 22 up to verse 16).

THE ART OF NEGOTIATION

It is widely accepted that Solomon was the wisest man that ever lived but when you look closely at his life we can also see that he was a shrewd businessman. He had an uncanny knack for identifying profitable ventures. So, in essence, his wisdom permeated to his business dealings. He was wise in managing the trade and finances of his kingdom. He emphasised the importance of diversification, strategic partnerships, and fair taxation. Subsequent kings were not so wise when it came to taxes (1 Kings 12:1-17).

We can adapt and apply Solomon's wisdom business practices to our modern day business strategies. In this way we can gain practical insights for success in today's world. When we explore the wisdom of Proverbs, we can apply them in a business context. Let's look at some key points:

Diversification

Solomon understood the importance of diversification. He invested in agriculture, mining, and trading. This practice ensured that his kingdom wealth was not tied to only one sector. He avoided over-reliance on any single source of income. This is a strategy that is often observed to resonate with modern portfolio diversification.

> Let us never negotiate out of fear. But let us never fear to negotiate.
> —John F. Kennedy

Strategic Partnerships

Solomon also knew the value of alliances. He formed alliances with neighbouring kingdoms to foster trade and economic growth. His maritime trade was particularly successful with his ships returning laden with exotic goods which further enriching his kingdom. This type of trade – transporting goods by sea – would have played a crucial role in his global supply chains and trade. This practice mirrors the importance of collaborations in today's globalised business environment.

Fair Taxation

King Solomon's taxation system in ancient Israel involved both a Poll Tax and an Income Tax. The Poll Tax was a per-person tax, often referred to as a "crossing over" levy, which may have been one of the earliest taxes in ancient Israel. The Income Tax was collected in the form of goods and services, rather than a monetary currency. This included provisions like flour, grains, cattle, sheep, and fowl.

Solomon's system of taxation was fair and just, ensuring the kingdom's treasury remained well-stocked without overburdening his subjects. This is a concept relevant to modern business taxation practices.

Infrastructure Investment
Solomon recognised the importance of infrastructure for a thriving economy. He believed that a kingdom's strength was in its people and their wellbeing. He invested in the things that they cared about. He built schools, hospitals and roads ensuring that his people had access to education, healthcare and sufficient transport. He also made other improvements to support trade and development.

Distribution of Wealth
King Solomon's wisdom extended to

the way he managed his treasury. Instead of hoarding his wealth, he believed in its circulation to stimulate the economy.

Proverbial Wisdom

Below are key verses from the book of Proverbs which provide wisdom focused business principles and can be used as practical guidance for financial success in your negotiations.

Proverbs 10:4 A slack hand causes poverty, but the hand of the diligent makes rich. This verse emphasises the importance of hard work and dedication in achieving success.

Proverbs 11:1 A false balance is an abomination to the Lord, but a just weight is his delight. This verse condemns dishonesty and fraud in business, emphasizing the need for integrity.

Proverbs 16:3: "Commit your work to the Lord, and your plans will be established." This verse suggests that faith and trust in God can lead to successful business endeavours.

Proverbs 21:5 The plans of the diligent lead surely to abundance, but everyone who is hasty comes only to poverty. This verse highlights the importance of thorough planning and diligence for business success.

Proverbs 14:23 All hard work brings a profit, but mere talk leads only to poverty. This verse emphasises the value of hard work and action over idle chatter.

Proverbs 16:8 Better to have little, with godliness, than to be rich and dishonest. This verse places integrity over wealth, suggesting that a moral compass is essential in business.

THE ART OF NEGOTIATION

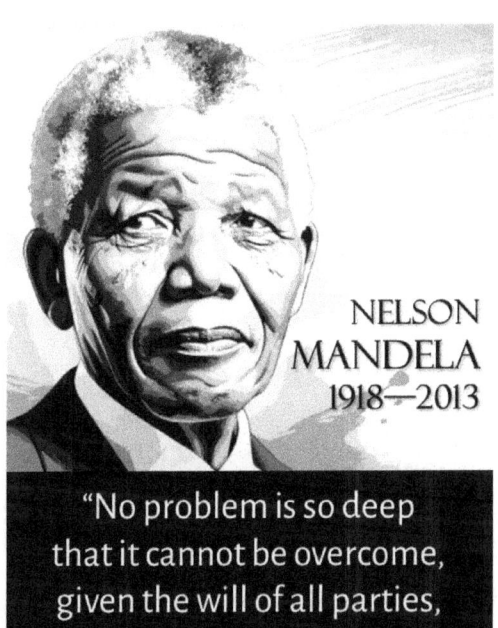

NELSON MANDELA
1918—2013

"No problem is so deep that it cannot be overcome, given the will of all parties, through discussion and negotiation rather than force and violence"

Appendix 1
Resources for Further Reading

"Getting to Yes"
Negotiating Agreement Without Giving In
by Roger Fisher and William Ury

"Never Split the Difference"
Negotiating as if Your Life Depended On It
by Chris Voss

"The Art of Negotiation"
How to Improvise Agreement in a Chaotic World"
by Michael Wheeler

"Solomon was a Businessman"
Advice from the Wealthiest Man on Earth
by Ardith & David W. Whitlock Baker

Appendix 2
Glossary of Negotiation Terms

BATNA: Best Alternative to a Negotiated Agreement; the best option available to a negotiator if negotiations fail.

Anchor: The initial offer made in a negotiation, which influences subsequent discussions.

Curb Appeal: The attractiveness of a property's exterior as perceived from the street.

Closing Costs: Fees and expenses incurred during the finalisation of a property transaction, including taxes, insurance, and agent commissions.

Comps: Comparable properties used as benchmarks to evaluate the value of a property being sold or purchased.

THE ART OF NEGOTIATION

By incorporating these resources and understanding the terminology, you can continue to enhance your negotiation skills and effectively navigate property transactions.

Thank you for joining me on this journey of exploration into the Art and Science of Negotiation!

THE ART OF NEGOTIATION

(Make a note of your own personal negotiation strategy key points)

_____

_____

_____

_____

_____

_____

_____

_____

_____

_____

_____

(Make a note of your own personal negotiation strategy key points)

_____
_____
_____
_____
_____
_____
_____
_____
_____
_____

THE ART OF NEGOTIATION

(Make a note of your own personal negotiation strategy key points)

_____
_____
_____
_____
_____
_____
_____
_____
_____
_____
_____

(Make a note of your own personal negotiation strategy key points)